MATISSE PRINTS

FROM THE MUSEUM OF MODERN ART

MATISSE PRINTS

FROM THE MUSEUM OF MODERN ART

THE FORT WORTH ART MUSEUM AND THE MUSEUM OF MODERN ART, NEW YORK • 1986

Published on the occasion of an exhibition organized by The Museum of Modern Art, New York, and shown at the Fort Worth Art Museum.

Edited by David Moorman, designed by Vicki Whistler, mechanicals by Jeanette Barber, typeset by Fort Worth Linotyping Co., Inc., printed by Anchor Press, Fort Worth.

Library of Congress Catalog Card Number 86-082223. ISBN 0-87070-439-7.

Cover: *Henri Matisse Engraving,* 1900–03
Drypoint
5 5/16 x 7 7/8 in. (15.1 x 20.1 cm.) D.1
Gift of Mrs. Bertram Smith

Frontispiece: *Dancer Reflected in the Mirror,* 1927
Transfer lithograph
15 5/8 x 11 in. (39.5 x 28.0 cm.) D.490
Gift of Abby Aldrich Rockefeller

Exhibition Schedule:

The Fort Worth Art Museum
Fort Worth, Texas
October 5–November 30, 1986

Art Museum of South Texas
Corpus Christi, Texas
January 3–February 28, 1987

The Winnipeg Art Gallery
Winnipeg, Manitoba
March 11–May 10, 1987

Cincinnati Art Museum
Cincinnati, Ohio
July 3–September 7, 1987

The Minneapolis Institute of Arts
Minneapolis, Minnesota
September 26–November 15, 1987

University of Iowa Museum of Art
Iowa City, Iowa
January 2–February 27, 1988

CONTENTS

FOREWORD

A world of intense color comes to mind when we first think of the art of Henri Matisse. Yet, as this exhibition title so aptly proves, Matisse's genius also conquered the graphic world of black on white. Here, in ninety-one prints, we follow his excitement in exploring the various printmaking media, and his delight in pursuing a wide range of themes.

Matisse Prints is the result of a collaboration between The Museum of Modern Art in New York and The Fort Worth Art Museum. It follows last year's *Surrealist Prints from the Collection of The Museum of Modern Art*, as the second joint venture to explore central aspects of the art of this century. The idea of *Matisse Prints from The Museum of Modern Art* was first proposed by Dr. Diane Upright, our former senior curator. Its creation has been undertaken by her colleague, Riva Castleman, director of the Department of Prints and Illustrated Books at the Modern: We owe her, especially, our fullest appreciation.

There were other key participants as well. Ms. Castleman and John Hallmark Neff, director of the Art Program and Art Advisor at The First National Bank of Chicago, each contributed an insightful essay on Matisse's prints, published here. Wendy Weitman, Ms. Castleman's assistant curator at the Modern, was of great assistance, as were two staff members in Fort Worth, James L. Fisher, curator of prints, and Ruth J. Hazel, curatorial associate.

This catalogue is also a collaboration, between Nancy Kranz, publications coordinator at The Museum of Modern Art, and Vicki Whistler, graphic designer at The Fort Worth Art Museum. David Moorman served as editor for this volume.

As did *Surrealist Prints*, *Matisse Prints from The Museum of Modern Art* will embark on an international tour following its première in Fort Worth. Betsy Jablow, the Modern's associate coordinator of exhibitions, arranged the travel of Matisse prints in the United States and in Canada. The entire exhibition was overseen by Dr. Upright and Ms. Castleman. To them, and to other staff members in New York and in Fort Worth who contributed to the show, we extend our grateful appreciation.

Finally, we again are especially grateful to the trustees of The Museum of Modern Art and that museum's director, Richard E. Oldenburg, for allowing these wonderful prints to create this special exhibition. By their generosity, we can again take joy in the world of Matisse.

E.A. Carmean, Jr., Director
The Fort Worth Art Museum

THE PRINTS OF MATISSE
by Riva Castleman,
Director of the Department of Prints and Illustrated Books,
The Museum of Modern Art

Matisse approached printmaking as an extension of drawing and occasionally as a form of relaxation after long periods of painting. Only twice did he think of his prints in terms of color, once in 1935 in an etched souvenir of the first version of his *Dance* mural (now in the Musée d'Art Moderne de la Ville de Paris), and again in 1950, in an aquatint that recapitulates *Young Girl in Green in Red Interior*, a painting dated three years earlier. The colored areas of the earlier print were made by the printer after a colored maquette, while in the later one the thickly brushed aquatinted black outline seems to be rather casually colored in. In his books, as well, Matisse largely disdained color — with the exceptions of *Jazz*, for which pochoir plates translated his collages of vividly colored paper, and *Poèmes de Charles d'Orléans*, which is decorated with reproductive lithographs from colored crayon drawings made for that purpose. Occasionally in his books, Matisse would have his linear crayon lithographs printed in brown or purple instead of black, and several of his linoleum cuts are printed in black on a terra-cotta ground—although this does not differ significantly from his use of *chine collé*, wherein the addition of a piece of grayish or creamy China paper under the composition of his etchings presents a different tone from the margins. Clearly, Matisse saw the various print techniques as the means of creating images in one color, and his preference was the black that varied from the modulations of drypoint to the constant thread of etching, from the soft furry stroke of a crayon and its smooth dissipation into grays to the profound darkness of monotype and linocut where the white lines of the images sing out, to the broadly brushed aquatints which make of black the liveliest color.

This selection consists of works printed in black. It begins with Matisse's first print, a self-portrait carefully constructed of drypoint lines, executed between 1900 and 1903, and it ends with the bold, aquatinted "masks" of 1951–52. In the half-century between these prints, Matisse made over 800 single etchings, drypoints, aquatints, woodcuts, lithographs, linocuts, and monotypes. For one extended period he made no single prints — between 1907 and 1913, when his painting evolved so spectacularly (from *Le Luxe* of 1907 to *The Red Studio* of 1911). In the early 1930s, when he worked on the *Dance* mural for Dr. Albert C. Barnes, and later, when World War II and his poor health restricted his activities, nearly all his printmaking focused upon the embellishment or illustration of books. Matisse's thinking about the properties of black and his use of them did not totally coalesce until after World War I. Nevertheless, from about 1906 he persisted in defining the figures in his paintings with black line, bringing different parts of the line into greater or lesser contrast with the color areas as the painting progressed. His attempts to perfect the balance of drawing and painting within one work continued throughout his life, culminating in the colored paper decoupages of the 1940s and 1950s, when the cut edges effectively replaced the black line.

During the first years of the century, Matisse's prints were largely sketched studies of models, the drypoint or needle being used like a pen to scratch out the parallel linear shading characteristic of academic work of the nineteenth century. The shadings and crosshatchings were also part of Matisse's drawing of the time, and they began to contribute to the spread of the image across the page, flattening the vestiges of perspective. More important than the rather docile nude studies is Matisse's self-portrait, which is partly experimental, with sketches at the edges of the plate that indicate the artist's ideas for how he would represent himself (one with a hat relates to a drawing of 1900) and several practice scratchings with various tools. The plate went through four stages, during which Matisse added more shading, particularly in the background and beneath the board upon which we see him steadying the copperplate while he scratches his likeness. For the final, published state of the print he has slightly reduced the size of the plate, and more important, he has burnished away some of the shading of the hands themselves. This makes his hands the focus of attention, and light seems to emanate from them.

As he so admired Rembrandt, Matisse might well have sought in his first attempt at printmaking to discover some of the means that the earlier master had used to achieve the illumination that often plays a prominent role in his engravings. Another possible influence in this print is the work of Odilon Redon, which Matisse admired. He also became acquainted with the older artist after purchasing two pastels by him in 1900. He must have been aware of the ways in which Redon used black and white to evoke the mysteries of Edgar Allan Poe and Charles Baudelaire. Indeed, Redon wrote of his method that it "proceeds naturally and easily from the vision of the mysterious world of shadows for which Rembrandt, in revealing it to us, supplied the key."[1]

It may be that Redon was also indirectly involved in one of the perplexing problems presented in Matisse's graphic work. Before the 1920s Matisse worked on a lithographic stone only once. That work, the *Large Nude* of 1906, is related to his other prints through the model's pose, which is the same in *The Large Woodcut* and *Small Light Woodcut* of the same year. What provokes concern about the *Large Nude* is its determined, volumetric rendering. There is nothing else like it in Matisse's work of the time. It has been dated 1904, 1906, 1907, and 1913, and because it was given two numbers in Matisse's print inventory, some have thought it may have been reworked at a later time. (Other lithographs were drawn on transfer paper which did not necessitate Matisse's appearance at the printer's.) What might have happened, however, suggested by the manner in which the artist worked his self-portrait, is that he experimented with refining the contours by drawing and scraping directly upon the stone, much as he did in his later charcoal drawings before he attempted a definitive rendering in ink or pencil. Like Matisse's transfer lithographs of the same period, the *Large Nude* was printed by Auguste Clot, but it was printed on a different paper, the China paper upon which Redon's portraits of 1900–08 were also printed, and this may indicate a connection between the two artists' projects. What points most directly to the 1906 date, however, is the similarity of the pose to that in *The Large Woodcut* and *Small Light Woodcut*, both datable to 1906 as they were exhibited at Galerie Druet in Paris early that year. Also, no drawings of the model in the same pose have been found after that year. The synthesized form of the seated nude in the lithograph rests within a shadowed background that echoes the compositional manner of several ink drawings of the time as well as that of the central figures in Matisse's important painting *Bonheur de vivre* (1905–06). In *The Large Woodcut* the expressively detailed figure is surrounded by a mass of lines that fill the background like magnetic waves, while in the *Small Black Woodcut* the lines meld together, providing the shadow that makes the figure more prominent, as in the lithograph.

For years there was a misunderstanding about the woodcuts, which, on the basis of a conversation with Matisse's wife in 1948, William S. Lieberman specified were linoleum cuts.[2] It was later discovered that the only surviving woodblock, that for *The Large Woodcut*, had been painted with blue and white paint, thus giving the appearance of something other than wood. This one block (for which there is an ink drawing that was used to transfer the composition to the block) was acquired by Frank Perls, the late art dealer, from the heirs of Ambroise Vollard in 1965, and sold by him to the Victoria and Albert Museum in 1976.[3] Most likely Ambroise Vollard, who had published albums of lithographs in the 1890s, had planned to issue an album of woodcuts by several artists, such as Matisse, Derain, Vlaminck, and Picasso. All these artists made woodcuts in or around 1906, and about that time Vollard induced several of them to make ceramics at the studio of André Methey. A ceramic plate decorated with a blue nude by Matisse in 1907 has also been cited as having similarities to the controversial lithograph referred to above.

Fortunately, there are no problems of this sort with Matisse's prints after this period. The fifteen transfer lithographs printed by Clot on creamy Japan paper in 1906 formed the foundation for the next series in 1913. The first group, associated with preparatory work for *Bonheur de vivre* and probably drawn from the same model, Rosa Arpino, did not lead to further involvement in printmaking. The eight of 1913 are directly related to three drypoints and three monotypes and they herald the beginning of a fertile period of printmaking.

Comparison between the transfer lithographs of 1906 and 1913 reveals that Matisse's mastery of the flowing, unbroken line as well as his almost instinctive capacity to place those lines in perfect relationship to the edges of the paper was developed to an extreme degree in those seven years. In the *Three-quarter Nude, Head Partly Showing*, he demonstrates his ability to fill the page with such exquisite balance that one accepts the near decapitation of the model as natural, because one feels that nothing whatsoever is lacking. This impression of completeness, fulfilled with only a few lines, is even clearer in the small monotype of 1915, *Standing Nude, Arms Crossed*.

Much of Matisse's intensive printmaking activity arose from having the means to take his own proofs in his studio. In November 1913 he set up a new studio in Paris and installed an etching press acquired that year. It was of this time that his daughter Marguerite Duthuit later recalled the activity of printing the monotypes which produced "a great moment of emotion at the instant when one discovered the imprint on the sheet of paper."[4] Running the press, which had to be done smoothly without stopping in order to impress the inked surface uniformly, was evidently a family task. Such recollections offer some glimpse of the environment in which Matisse worked on the many etchings of his family, models, and friends during the first years of World War I. Among them were the wives of André Derain and Demetrius Galanis, who had been left alone in Paris when their husbands went to war. While painting a portrait of Yvonne Landsberg, Matisse made several etchings of her as well as her brother's friend, the English philosopher and Byzantine scholar Matthew Prichard. Walter Pach, the American painter, had his portrait etched while he was arranging for an exhibition of Matisse's work (including twenty-five etchings) to be shown at the opening of the Montross Gallery in New York in January 1915. The painter Juan Gris needed money, so his wife joined the intimate community as a model. Among the many small portrait etchings made at this time were two, one of Fanny Galanis, the other, a double portrait of Josette Gris, which were sold to raise money so that Mme Matisse could make food and clothing packages for relatives and friends interned by the Germans who had occupied Matisse's mother's hometown of Bohain.[5]

Unlike the startling original painting of Yvonne Landsberg that Matisse completed in 1914, in which the abstracting tendencies he presented in his canvasses of 1913–16 reached an early climax, the intimate etchings of the same sitter incorporate elements that endured thereafter in the artist's repertoire. It was not until 1914

that Matisse began to etch his plates instead of scratching his lines with drypoint. The unmodulated etched line remained on one plane, the plate's surface, and encouraged some attempts at composition that would extend the image to the edge of the plate. The first use of leaves and flowers surrounding the face or figure occurs in the etched portraits of Yvonne Landsberg and others in 1914 and in one drypoint of Mme Matisse. The surrounding foliage gives to the Landsberg etching a faint prettiness that is absent in the painting, but the mood anticipates the considerable changes his work would take, beginning in 1916, when he began to spend long periods in Nice.

In 1922 the print publisher Frapier sent stones to several artists, requesting that they produce a lithograph for an album he had planned. With his *Model Resting,* Matisse embarked upon a direction in printmaking that served him throughout the twenties. In this case he drew (for only the second time directly upon stone) in the shaded, modelled manner that was to characterize even his transfer lithographs thereafter. The sexily languorous representation of his model Henriette is related to specific paintings; the method would be repeated when such complete compositions were forthcoming. Although only a hint of the abundance of decorative fabrics used as wall hangings, draperies, and clothing appears in this print, the use of various natural and geometric designs that they offer gives contrast and texture to the soft rendering and emphasizes the play of light upon the nude body. This device is used

Nude with Blue Cushion Beside a Fireplace, 1925
Transfer lithograph
25⅛ x 18⅞ in. (63.8 x 48.0 cm.) D.454
Gift of Abby Aldrich Rockefeller

to even greater effect in the *Large Odalisque in Striped Pantaloons*, a transfer litho-graph of Henriette of 1925. Several transfer lithographs of 1924, including *Nude with Blue Cushion Beside a Fireplace*, present a nude, seated upon an armchair with one leg raised and hands folded above her head, looking somewhat obliquely at the spectator. They are part of an entire program of works, both painting and sculp-ture, utilizing this pose that evolved from a renewed interest in Michelangelo's sculpture for the Medici tomb which Matisse drew from casts in 1918. In the *Large Odalisque* of 1925, however, the arms are dropped, the face is more exposed, and the introduced patterns are restricted to two: the draped chair and the emphatically striped pantaloons. More important, however, is the positioning of the chair, which has been put into greater prominence by darkening the background. Not only does the model confront the viewer more boldly because of the frontal disposition of the chair, but the simplification and near symmetry of the setting create an effect of monumentality. Against this substantial structure the impression of the sitter's satiny flesh vacillates between sensuous pliancy and dignified solidity.

After 1925 and the departure of Henriette, Matisse continued to create litho-graphs in this soft, shaded style—among them, the highly finished *Dancer Reflected in the Mirror* (1927) and *The White Fox* (1929), his stylish portrait of the model Lisette.[6] He did not discontinue, however, the type of linear transfer lithograph that characterized his early work, but transformed it with some bits and pieces of local shading, as in the *Arabesque* of 1924 and *Upside-down Nude with Stove* of 1929. Both works are essentially linear, but with the addition of pattern that brought the figure into an equivalent relationship with its surroundings, it seemed necessary to provide hints of different intensities of color. This was often accomplished by drawing large areas with the side of his crayon.

In order to understand the importance of Matisse's linear work in the 1920s, which significantly prepared him for several ambitious projects in the 1930s, it is necessary to study his drypoints and etchings of 1929. Only a few copperplate prints were made between 1915 and 1929, and the most interesting of those are drypoints in which a half-clothed figure is seated amongst a lavish array of floral materials. The placement of these models in the compositions — consistently cut off at one extremity or more, and composed of lines that pick out the forms in a sort of shorthand — makes the entire rectangle of each print an unmodulated series of shapes. The pattern's tendency to fly out is pinned down by the occasional sets of parallel lines, widened strokes, or strings of dark beads which act as intensified black anchors.

In 1929 Matisse made over a hundred etchings and drypoints, continuing to present in many of these small works a kind of mosaic of linear elements. In a series of Oriental women shown against a tiled wall, he has concentrated on moving the focal point of the composition to the upper half of the drawing, where the business of facial features melds with a consistent pattern of tiles. Another set of prints plays with unusual angles of viewing the nude subject. Like the lithograph *Upside-down Nude with Stove* of the same year, the etching *Study of Upside-down Nude* is filled with flowers, wavy lines, and busy objects that occupy with their variable weights the spaces around the model. Unlike the lithograph, there is no shading and the patterns alone distribute the movement within the composition. The oddly contorted figure stares up and out, reminiscent of one of Matisse's earliest lithographs of 1906, but examination of the few lines that make up the features of the face reveals how carefully only a few have been selected to represent the whole. Economy, a positive epithet for the abstracting tendency in Matisse's drawing, is not necessarily descriptive of what he accomplishes. Often the detail selected is not the one normally preferred to represent, for instance, an eye. It is the placement of the mark that indicates what it means in Matisse's work, rather than a selection from what is available. That this has been interpreted as an art of signs is not unexpected, but those signs emanate from a hand that has repeated all of them so extensively that they are brought to occupy their significant places almost subconsciously.

In *Study of Upside-down Nude* there is a bowl of goldfish. An entire group of prints is devoted to a girl watching goldfish in a bowl. In *Young Woman with Black Eyes, Staring at an Aquarium* the model is not merely amused by the fish, but transfixed. Her right eye, the darkest area in the etching, echoes the outline of the fish head at the extreme right edge of the plate, identifying for the viewer the exact meaning of the unadorned bent line and concentric circles that are all the artist has offered. In this series nearly everything has been simplified to the utmost. That

Matisse chose to center his concentration upon a goldfish bowl, which, according to some historians, he was the first artist to use, helps to focus the poetic goals that are implicit in his graphic work.

Early in 1930 Matisse left the Eastern Hemisphere for the first time for a trip to America and Tahiti. A few years earlier he had made the acquaintance of Tériade, who asked him to illustrate Stéphane Mallarmé's poetry for an associate, the publisher Albert Skira, around 1930.[7] Upon his return from Tahiti he began to work both on the book and on his large mural of the *Dance* for Barnes's home in Merion, Pennsylvania. The twenty-nine etchings that Matisse made to decorate the pages of Skira's Mallarmé resulted from dozens of drawings. In some cases the images are relatively literal: the artist did not think in terms of pure illustration but rather the visual impression of each page which he laid out, both image and text, in the manner of his mural. From his many etchings and drypoints of 1929 Matisse learned how to balance thin lines against empty spaces, and in his description of his prints for Mallarmé he pointed out, "The design fills the page without a margin so that the page stays light, because the design is not, as usual, massed toward the center but spreads out over the whole page."[8] The lightness or whiteness of the full-page etchings was meant to draw the reader's attention, before the reading of the visually darker text. In contrast to most of Matisse's etchings, the majority of the Mallarmé prints were done from memory or photographs, most references to the model arising from drawings considerably removed from the moment of etching.

With the exception of the soft-ground etchings he made from tracing drawings for James Joyce's *Ulysses* (Limited Editions Club, 1935), Matisse completed only a few plates before the outbreak of World War II. Beginning in 1945, all his etchings were portraits or stylized faces. A series of fourteen such line etchings of a woman from Martinique were studies for the frontispiece of Baudelaire's *Les Fleurs du mal* published in 1947. In many cases several nearly identical etchings were created in order to achieve one that might enhance a book of poetry or essays by one of his friends. In 1946, the year that most of these linear heads were etched, he created the first of his aquatint "masks." In these disembodied heads, ciphers made from a few strokes of an ink-laden brush, the contrast of black and white becomes dazzling as lines broaden in width but diminish in number. Finally, in 1951–52 Matisse made his last prints, the three masks in *To Friendship*, produced to illustrate a book on Guillaume Apollinaire by André Rouveyre. In six aquatint studies the oval heads of Apollinaire, Rouveyre, and Matisse hang together in a humorous, symbolic relationship.

The thick brushstrokes that have, in the granular surface of aquatint, such extraordinarily palpable intensity, evolved from the flowing calligraphy of Matisse's handwritten pages in the book *Jazz*, completed around 1946, published in 1947. The writing was meant to present an equivalency to the brilliant colored compositions opposite it. This balance, in which black and white in their most extreme contrast are played against equally extreme color groupings, was one he wished to achieve in his Chapel of the Rosary (". . . my chief aim was to balance a surface of

Pages 128–129
from *Poésies* by Stéphane Mallarmé
Lausanne: Albert Skira & Cie., 1932
Etchings
13 1/16 x 9 15/16 in. (33.2 x 25.3 cm.)
The Louis E. Stern Collection

light and color against a solid wall with black drawing on a white background.")[9] The aquatint heads are easily related to the sweeping black drawings on tile in the chapel, and they take on a similar role in their relationship to the colors of any environment.

The theme of how Matisse used black has run through this survey of his printed work like the ground bass of Baroque music. During World War I, he made black a major subject of several paintings, stating later, "I began to use pure black as a color of light and not as a color of darkness."[10] Concurrently, he produced a great variety of monotypes, themselves nearly entirely black, with only wisps of white picking out portraits, nudes, and still lifes (very few still lifes appear among his prints). It is possible that Matisse's fascination with white line on black at this time arose from his interest in the type of Coptic weaving in which figures are depicted in solid, dark purple with features picked out in white. One way to evoke this effect was to take a solidly inked plate and draw extremely fine furrows into the ink. The retention of pure lines in Matisse's monotypes during the process of printing was often as erratic as their appearance in the Coptic weaving. He explored this aspect of monotype in two ways: some complete compositions or details were drawn lightly, so that when printed, they presented a rather effervescent appearance; others were drawn with strong, confident strokes which printed clearly, cleaving the black like flashes of lightning. In 1936 Matisse attempted to work again in white on black and created several aquatints in this manner, one of which was to be added to deluxe copies of an issue of *Cahiers d'art*. Another, very much in the style

Pages 58 and 59
from *Pasiphaé / Chant de Minos*
by Henry de Montherlant
Paris: Martin Fabiani, 1944
Linoleum cuts
12⅞ x 9¾ in. (32.7 x 24.8 cm.)
The Louis E. Stern Collection

of Coptic figuration, is the oddly shaped — for Matisse — frieze of *Five Female Heads,* sketched after his daughter Marguerite in 1939.[11]

When Matisse began to make linocuts, treated once more as white line on black, his gouging generally was quite assured. The slightly swelling lines were infrequently accented with repetitive dashes that outlined petals of flowers or other "soft" imagery. He began to work in this medium in 1938 and completed twenty-six editions that year. In 1941 he began to cut the blocks for his ambitious decoration of Henry de Montherlant's *Pasiphaé / Chant de Minos,* published in 1944. In all, the artist cut hundreds of blocks for this project, not only several variations on each subject he had planned for full pages, but also the initials, heading bands, and other purely decorative elements. Those additional ornaments were printed in red, and their function within the composition of each set of pages is essentially that of signals for beginnings and endings. The red initials occur at specific places in the text where a "passionate sequence" in the voice of Minos or the voice of Pasiphaé or her nurse begins.[12] They are treated like the black prints, their solid tone punctuated with white lines, and they act as ballast so that the strings of text will hold their own against the ponderous blackness of the single-page linocuts. In 1946 the amateur violinist Matisse wrote of his linoleums, "I have often thought that this simple medium is comparable to the violin with its bow: a surface, a gouge — four taut strings and a swatch of hair. The gouge, like the violin bow, is in direct rapport with the feelings of the engraver: the slightest distraction in the tracing of a line causes a slight involuntary pressure of the fingers on the gouge and has an adverse effect on the line. Likewise, a change in the pressure of the fingers which hold the bow of a violin is sufficient to change the character of the sound from soft to loud."[13]

Relating line to sound, Matisse thus accentuated the abstract foundation of his work. For nearly his entire creative career he persisted in using line as the main channel for his spirit.[14] In his prints, as in those very earliest examples on China paper, the basic material was black. Since the most ancient times, when its usable charcoal form was born from fire, black has been imbued with a magical element. From written symbols to print, photograph, and film, black (with it usual companion, white) has represented reality where it clearly does not depict it. Like most emerging painters at the beginning of the twentieth century, Matisse eschewed color when he worked on prints. It was not only the way of Rembrandt that he followed, but also the way of expressing new ideas. When he first drew figures and excluded all elements but an unbroken line, it was to produce lithographs. With black ink alone Matisse created a new and enchanted galaxy.

NOTES

[1]Odilon Redon, "Suggestive Art, 1909," *Theories of Modern Art,* ed. Herschel B. Chipp (Berkeley and Los Angeles: University of California Press, 1968), p. 119.

[2]William S. Lieberman, *Matisse: 50 Years of His Graphic Art* (New York: George Braziller, Inc., 1956), p. 19.

[3]Lumley Cazalet Ltd. advertisement, *Print Quarterly,* Vol. III, No. 2 (June 1986), unpaginated.

Marguerite G. Duthuit, letter to author, March 24, 1978.

[4]Marguerite G. Duthuit, letter to author, March 7, 1978.

[5]Claude Duthuit, letter to author, June 4, 1986.

[6]Françoise Garnaud, note to author, [June 1986].

[7]Michel Anthonioz, ed., *Hommage à Tériade,* exhibition catalogue (Paris: Grand Palais, 1973), p. 16.

[8]Alfred H. Barr, Jr., *Matisse: His Art and His Public* (New York: The Museum of Modern Art, 1951), p. 244.

[9]Henri Matisse, "The Chapel of the Rosary, 1951," *Matisse on Art,* ed. Jack D. Flam (New York: Phaedon Press, Ltd., 1973), p. 128.

[10]Barr, op. cit., p. 190.

[11]Claude Duthuit, conversation with the author, June 12, 1986.

[12]Pierre Schneider, *Matisse* (New York: Rizzoli, 1984), p. 259.

[13]Henri Matisse, "How I Made My Books, 1946," *Matisse on Art,* p. 109.

[14]Henri Matisse, "Letter to Henry Clifford, 1948," *Matisse on Art,* p. 121.

HENRI MATISSE: NOTES ON HIS EARLY PRINTS

by John Hallmark Neff
Director of the Art Program and Art Advisor
The First National Bank of Chicago

This exhibition gives us the first major look at Matisse's prints since 1983, when Matisse's daughter Marguerite Duthuit-Matisse and her son Claude Duthuit published *Henri Matisse: catalogue raisonné de l'oeuvre gravé*. This massive two-volume catalogue lists and illustrates the 829 known etchings, drypoints, lithographs, woodcuts, linocuts, aquatints, and monotypes produced by Matisse over a span of five decades.[1]

To some degree this situation reflects our obsession with the unique object. We mistakenly assume that we can see his graphic work anytime. Our concentration is thus continually postponed. In fact, only a few museums have even a small fraction of Matisse's prints; only three or four can claim the number or variety to mount an exhibition such as this, and no collection is complete.[2]

Except for their physical dimensions or their papers, much of what is known about the prints has been ascertained after the fact, especially in regard to the work before 1922. Unlike today's lavish workshop editions, which arrive with elaborate brochures documenting the most minute details of materials, procedures, and personnel, Matisse's prints carried only basic information—his signature, his notation of the kind or number of the impression, and the size of the edition. Sometimes he added a personal dedication to a friend, but he never indicated the year, let alone the month or day when he made them. The titles now attached to most of the prints—as well as those of many of his other works—are descriptive afterthoughts appended by dealers, family, friends, and even critics and art historians. With few exceptions, we have very little precise information about the circumstances of how or why a particular image or group of images came to be.[3]

That is why the following remarks focus on two groups of prints from 1913 and 1914, in the hope that precise details may help to clarify our understanding of other prints in this exhibition.

For example, the two etched portraits of the extraordinary Matthew Stewart Prichard[4] are described as "probably having been made from memory or from a photograph" because the Englishman, on a study trip to Germany in August 1914, had been interned as an enemy alien shortly after the declaration of war.[5] On the contrary, one of Prichard's letters tells us that Matisse apparently started sketching with an etching in mind as early as November 3, 1913, and very likely made the prints themselves the following June, when Prichard was still very much in Paris.[6] The following excerpt, from his extensive and informative correspondence with Isabella Stewart Gardner in Boston, evokes the ambiance of Matisse's studio and it is worth remembering when looking at the many other etched portraits of family and visitors that Matisse made around that time:

> Matisse is very lively: I was in his studio yesterday where there were as many as twelve people. He has finished a great portrait of his wife[7] and two other pictures lately: he has done some good etchings too. Did I tell you that he is doing a book-plate too for my friends at Oxford? He has made one or two sketches for it. He thinks he will be able to express in it a feeling he has already found utterance for but never to the point of conveying the full meaning of its intensity.[8]

In another letter, July 12, 1914, he reports that Matisse "has just finished a wonderful portrait of a girl," referring to the much-discussed portrait, *Mlle Yvonne Landsberg*, now in the Philadelphia Museum of Art.[9] We know that Matisse had commenced his many drawings for her portrait by first making countless studies of magnolia blossoms, buds, and leaves which had reminded him of the shy young

Brazilian girl, still in her teens.[10] He also made three etchings and two drypoints.[11] With the completion date of her painted portrait fixed to the first two weeks of July, and with Prichard's two etched portraits dated with some assurance to June, it is reasonable to suggest that the six other etchings with borders of magnolia leaves or flowers were all done about the same time, in June 1914.[12] In the case of Prichard, however, the symbolic magnolias may well have had more than decorative significance, for it was he who had taken Mlle Landsberg's brother to meet Matisse and thereby instigated (and undoubtedly encouraged) the eventual commission.

The Prichard etchings and the other small portraits were essentially made for private reasons. Pulled in small editions of fifteen or fewer prints, they were not made for sale so much as to circulate among the coterie of friends and family members depicted.[13] This seems not to have been the intention with the many prints of female nudes, however, a subject to which Matisse always returned, and he returned because he considered the human figure the foundation of his drawing and therefore of his art.

In the March 1914 issue of their new *Bulletin,* the gallery Bernheim-Jeune alerted their clients to the availability of "Les estampes d'Henri Matisse," thirty-three in all, twenty-nine of these identifiable from the descriptions as nudes. The prints were grouped in the simple catalogue by year, medium, and with descriptive or generic titles, detailed dimensions and edition sizes. A note at the end reassured the potential connoisseur that all the plates had been crossed out after printing.[14] This modest list may well be the first published attempt to document Matisse's early prints. It was probably assembled by the gallery director, Félix Fénéon, more than likely with the artist's help.[15] Following a distinguished and often controversial career as an art critic, during which he championed Seurat and the Neo-Impressionists, Redon and the Symbolists, and other young artists, Fénéon came to the gallery to establish its modern art department in 1906. It was Fénéon who brought the rising Matisse into the gallery, officially in 1909, but actually several years before.

Their close relationship is relevant here because some of the dates given for several key prints in the 1914 *Bulletin* would place those prints significantly later in Matisse's development than the dates given by more recent sources. Matisse's self-portrait, together with all the other earliest drypoints, is dated to 1906, not 1900–1903. And the always problematic *Large Nude* lithograph is listed not from 1906, but from the year preceding the catalogue, 1913.[16]

Although there are other details in this early catalogue which do not seem accurate in light of other documents,[17] its close proximity in time, place, and circumstance to the artist himself make it a source which must be taken into serious account.

Less controversially, it specifically dates to 1913 the second group of drypoints, which includes the series of nudes, *Half-length Nude* being one example. It also dates to 1913 the second series of eight transfer lithographs, which for many years were assumed to be from 1914. This group of figure studies contains some of the

classic prints of this century. The concision, spontaneity, and elegance of these deceptively simple drawings, their placement within the four edges of the paper, and the variety of often unexpected poses is more sophisticated than all but a few of the lithographs of nudes from 1906. Larger than these, and printed in fifty rather than twenty-five impressions, the 1913 lithographs were also developed around a single model. She posed for *Half-length Nude* and at least two related drypoints, perhaps six monotypes, and at least one painting.[18]

Identified only as "G. R." in the 1982 Fribourg catalogue (the most extensive exhibition to date of Matisse's graphic work),[19] she is not mentioned in the *catalogue raisonné*. However, two recently exhibited drawings confirm her name: Germaine Raynal, wife of the art critic Maurice Raynal.[20] Ironically, he was a staunch supporter of Picasso and the Cubists and was openly hostile to Matisse in his reviews. The model's long torso and neck, distinctive breasts and coiffure — particularly her bangs — are readily identifiable in the works cited above. Yet so also is her face, and it is much more lively and expressive than what we usually expect from Matisse's figure drawings. Some of his prints of Germaine Raynal, *Nude in Rocking Chair* and *Black Eyes* and *Half-length Nude*, also qualify as portraits.

By all accounts, she modeled for Matisse during the winter of 1913–14, though it is uncertain when she actually arrived or how long she stayed. What is clear is that she was established as one of Matisse's regular models well before the events of August 1914 brought other wives of art-world figures into the Matisse household and studio where he made many drawings and etchings of them, such as *Mme Derain*. Apparently Matisse paid them for these sittings as a small way of helping financially while their husbands were away at the Front. The chronology helps to explain why only Madame Raynal is depicted in the nude.

Finally, it may be that her close friendship with both Matisse and Juan Gris (who painted her in 1912) was the link which led to the artists' eventful discussions

when they found themselves together in Collioure, in September 1914, awaiting news about the war. There has been much interesting speculation that the "relent-less" philosophical exchanges between Matisse and the young Cubist might in part explain a more severe, linear organization of the surface which subsequently appeared in some of Matisse's work.[21] However that may be, the only print even remotely reflecting this stylistic shift is, appropriately, one of seven etched studies of Josette Gris which Matisse made in Paris later that fall.

This particular example tends to reinforce the view that Matisse's prints were at this time primarily diversions from his painting, a nevertheless demanding—and eventually profitable—form of relaxation. It might be accurate to say that while Matisse made prints he was not really a printmaker, not a printmaker in the technical sense because most of his prints were direct transcriptions of his drawing with needle or crayon. With few exceptions, he didn't rework his images through successive states. The major exception, printed in four variations, was the *Self-Portrait*; but from what we know about Matisse's practice when teaching himself the fundamentals of a new medium, it is significant that this drypoint is generally considered to be his first.

For lithography he much preferred drawing on transfer paper to working directly with the stone. Many of the 1913 prints of Germaine Raynal are almost indistinguishable from separate drawings made with the litho crayon.[22] By prevailing standards, Matisse was taking shortcuts with the medium; transfer paper had been invented to expedite the transfer of the basic sketch to the lithographic stone, which the artist was then supposed to work up in detail in all the traditional ways. The transfer paper design was not originally intended to be an end in itself, and it wasn't until the 1920s that Matisse exploited the full potential of the technique, when the rich tonal gradations he demanded could only be achieved with the scraper and glass paper. Except for the monotypes that were, of necessity, printed quickly by Matisse or his children, the fact remains that he demonstrated little interest in the craft of printmaking. The love of arcane recipes for grounds and special inks was not for him. He much preferred to leave the printing details to specialists. Even the three major woodcuts of 1906 — the only prints he ever showed in the Salon — were printed from blocks meticulously cut by Madame Matisse, and then only after her husband's brush and ink designs had been carefully reversed so as to preserve their original appearance.

This is not to imply that Matisse was indifferent to his materials or that he didn't enjoy the excitement of waiting to see how his drawings might respond to the uncertainties of the printing process — the humidity, or the idiosyncrasies of his small press. In fact we know that he did, particularly when preparing his illustrated books. But his real interest was in the initial act of drawing, and while he respected the differences between drawings and prints he made very little distinction between them, starting to work afresh on a new plate as though working through the pages of a sketchbook. That a drawing was also an etching or drypoint simply raised the stakes by introducing the impersonal, abstracting effects of the acid on his line, to say nothing of the reversed image itself, as unexpected sometimes as though created by his other hand. With the success of each design depending on the perfect placement of very few lines, each having to carry the significance of the observed form as Matisse identified with it, there was for each print an undeniable element of risk. This process was played out at its most extreme in the monotypes. Each one was technically a "print" but it was also unique, and that may suggest why Matisse did not make more of them.

Having lived with two of the lithographs for fourteen years—a torso from 1913 evoked by thirty-two linear notations and a 1922 nude developed from thousands —I still find each a source of continuing discovery. Each in its way is a reminder of an old truism about Matisse: that when one isolates a detail which at first appears distorted or even ugly, one soon realizes that without it the overall composition would be too perfect, without life. In his prints, no less than in his drawings, he created these "mistakes" to show us a reality more complete than one we might be tempted to impose.

NOTES

[1]Marguerite Duthuit-Matisse, Claude Duthuit, *Henri Matisse: catalogue raisonné de l'oeuvre gravé*, in collaboration with Françoise Garnaud, with preface by Jean Guichard-Meili (Paris: 1983). Hereafter, "Duthuit" or "D." refers to the catalogue number. The hundreds of other graphics that Matisse made for book illustrations will appear in a forthcoming volume.

[2]The most extensive holdings of Matisse prints are those of the Cabinet des Estampes of the Bibliothèque Nationale, Paris. These include many of the one- or two-of-a-kind impressions donated by members of the Matisse family. In addition to The Museum of Modern Art, New York, the Baltimore Museum of Art has an extensive collection of the prints, including studies and maquettes for *Poésies de Stéphane Mallarmé* (1932) in the Cone Collection. The Department of Drawings and Prints at the Victoria and Albert Museum, London, has numerous etchings and prints, as well as ninety-five lithographs, all but four of them acquired directly from Madame Duthuit in 1935.

[3]Much of the information we have concerning the prints can be found in the following sources: Alfred H. Barr, Jr., *Matisse: His Art and His Public* (New York: The Museum of Modern Art, 1951); William S. Lieberman, *Matisse: 50 Years of His Graphic Art* (New York: George Braziller, 1956); Jean Guichard-Meili, "Matisse et la splendeur de blanc," *Matisse: l'oeuvre gravé* (Paris: Bibliothèque Nationale, 1970); Guichard-Meili, "Couleurs de blanc, lumières du noir," *Matisse: Donation Jean Matisse* (Paris: Bibliothèque Nationale, 1981). Also see Guichard-Meili's preface to the *catalogue raisonné*. Barr gives an account of Walter Pach's etched portrait, pp. 186–87. Pach is quoted at length in Lieberman.

For drawings: Dominique Fourcade, "'Je crois qu'en dessin j'ai pu dire quelque chose,'" *Henri Matisse: dessins et sculpture* (Paris: Musée Nationale d'Art Moderne, 1975); John Elderfield, *The Drawings of Henri Matisse*, introduction by John Golding, catalogue by Magdalena Dobrowski (New York: The Museum of Modern Art, 1985).

For prints and drawings: Barr, *Matisse: His Art and His Public*; John Elderfield, et al., *Matisse in the Collection of The Museum of Modern Art* (New York: The Museum of Modern Art, 1978). Elderfield includes detailed commentaries on drawings and prints by William S. Lieberman and Riva Castleman.

[4]Prichard (1865–1936), museum man, archaeologist, and linguist, left the Boston Museum to reside in Paris, where he attended the philosopher Henri Bergson's lectures. He evidently discussed Bergson at length with Matisse, and he discusses Bergson's ideas in his letters to Mrs. Gardner. Prichard was adamant on the role of religion in the creation of art, particularly Byzantine art, and it was he who introduced a young Byzantinist, Georges Duthuit, into the Matisse household. Duthuit later married Matisse's daughter Marguerite. See Alfred H. Barr, op. cit., p. 105, and Pierre Schneider, *Matisse* (New York: Rizzoli, 1984), pp. 732–33.

[5]Duthuit, op. cit. D.43.

[6]Matthew Stewart Prichard–Isabella Stewart Gardner Correspondence, Isabella Stewart Gardner Museum, Boston. The first letter (November 4, 1913) does not specify that the sketches are of Prichard, but in context it seems clear that this is what he meant. A letter to Mrs. Gardner of April 10, 1920, begins: "It was very gratifying to know that you found something in the little Matisse etching. It was made in June 1914 . . ." The reference is to his portrait (D.44), which his friend Thomas Whittemore had just delivered to Mrs. Gardner; the etching, and another of Irene Vignier, are in the museum's collection (confirmed by Karen Haas of the Gardner staff, August 7, 1986).

[7]The painting is clearly *Portrait of the Artist's Wife*, the last painting to be acquired by Matisse's Russian patron Sergei Shchukin, now in The Hermitage Museum, Leningrad. Illustrated in *Henri Matisse: Paintings and Sculptures in Soviet Museums* (Leningrad: Aurora, 1978), Catalogue No. 51 and notes, pp. 180–81.

[8]Prichard–Gardner CSS, letter of November 4, 1913.

[9]Prichard–Gardner CSS, letter of July 12, 1914.

[10]Barr, op. cit., pp. 184–85 and notes. Barr's discussion of the painted portrait, notable for the curved lines radiating out from the figure, suggests the possibility of Bergson's influence and mentions that Mlle Landsberg and her brother had attended Bergson's lectures at the Collège de France with Prichard. In a letter to Mrs. Gardner (December 18, 1910), Prichard paraphrases Bergson as saying, "the great portrait painter reached the reality of his subject, his rhythm, and it was there that the painting touched music."

[11]D.31–35.

[12]D.24, D.27, D.30, D.33, D.39, D.40.

[13]Barr, op. cit., p. 186, says that "Apparently Matisse planned to publish the series or a selection from it in an album, but in the end those that were published were issued separately . . ." (presumably on the basis of information from the artist or his family).

[14]Archives, Galerie Bernheim-Jeune, Paris.

[15]The catalogue is listed in a critical biography of his writings in *Félix Fénéon: au-delà de l'impressionisme,* ed. Françoise Cachin (Paris: Hermann, 1966), p. 181.

[16]The last item in the *Bulletin* catalogue listed under 1913 as No. 8, the single lithograph, can be identified as the *Large Nude* by its dimensions, edition size, and paper (*chine-chine*). Barr, op. cit., p. 99 and note 7, discusses the dating for *Large Nude*, noting that it is "usually dated 1907 and sometimes included in the early series from which it differs completely in style, more closely resembling such abstract figures as those in the big painting, *Bathers by a River.*" Somewhat reluctantly, he accepts the 1907 date for "this unique stone." In his account of *Bathers by a River* (p. 190 and note 8), he discusses the possibility that Matisse worked on it in 1913 and even 1910 before finishing it in 1916–17. This has been confirmed (see the author's "Matisse and Decoration: The Shchukin Panels," *Art in America,* LXIV, No. 4, July–August, 1975, p. 45 and note), leaving the possibility that Barr's analogy might provide a basis for dating the lithograph circa 1913. He was apparently unaware of the *Bulletin* catalogue. The case against 1913, however, could be made with the self-portrait drypoint as the analogy. If we assume Matisse's first prints in each new medium were somewhat tentative and traditional, allowing him to try out the full range of techniques, then both the *Large Nude* and the self-portrait qualify. Because we have a group of figure lithographs to confirm his activity circa 1906, we may surmise that the *Large Nude* comes from Matisse's initial period of contact with lithographic stone, and that the experience of working it might have encouraged him to simplify his approach by using transfer paper — just as he moved from the crosshatchings of his early drypoints to simple contours. Suggestions that *Large Nude* was begun circa 1906 and (like *Bathers by a River*) taken up later, circa 1913, would indeed account both for his self-instruction and for the actual appearance of the print.

On another matter, the *Bulletin* catalogue confirms Barr's contention that although he had seen photographs or originals of ten of the series of 1906 lithographs, only, "half a dozen are commonly met with." Duthuit lists twelve as a coherent group (D.391–402) but the *Bulletin* mentions seven, indicating that all may not have been equally available.

[17]For example, the three woodcuts (D.317–319) and the first group of lithographs are dated to 1907, despite the fact that the catalogue for Matisse's one-man show at the Galerie Druet, in March 1906, concludes with "Dessins, aquarelles, lithographies et gravures sur bois." A year later at the Salon des Indépendants, Matisse showed three "gravures sur bois" (Nos. 5244–5246). There is no proof that the 1906 reference to woodcuts necessarily refers to the three we know best today; there may have been others, as a newly discovered small one (D.320) suggests. Even if the *Bulletin* is mistaken here, the variance is only one year, while the self-portrait drypoint and the *Large Nude* lithograph are dated fully six years later.

[18]See D.11–13, D.321–326, respectively. The painting is *Gray Nude with Bracelet,* cited by Riva Castleman in John Elderfield, et al., *Matisse in the Collection of The Museum of Modern Art,* p. 102; also illustrated in *Henri Matisse: exposition de centenaire* (Paris: 1970), Catalogue No. 120.

[19]*Henri Matisse, gravures et lithographies* (Fribourg: Musée d'Art et d'Histoire, 1982), Nos. 370–372.

[20]John Elderfield, *The Drawings of Henri Matisse,* notes for Catalogue Nos. 28 and 29 citing Madame Duthuit. He also cites Madame Duthuit concerning the other prints in question.

[21]Douglas Cooper, *The Cubist Epoch* (London: Phaidon, 1970), p. 207.

[22]A drawing in lithographic crayon, identical in every detail to *Visage à la frange* (and D.413) was sold at Sotheby's, London, on June 25, 1986 ("Impressionist and Modern Drawings and Watercolours," Lot 394). Described as "the study for the lithograph of 1913," it looks to be the actual drawing (on transfer paper?) from which the lithographs were eventually derived, including the artist's initials at lower left. The fact that using transfer paper did not necessarily destroy the original drawing nor reverse the final image certainly recommended its use to Matisse. The author has not seen the original of this drawing. It was authenticated by Madame Duthuit. Another drawing in litho crayon is illustrated in "Henri Matisse: An Exhibition of Selected Drawings in Homage to Frank Perls" (Los Angeles / San Francisco: John Berggruen Gallery / Margo Leavin Gallery, 1975), No. 4, identified as *Nu assis avec les jambes croisées,* 1913. It is another study of Germaine Raynal, probably made with a lithograph in mind.

SELECTED ILLUSTRATIONS

1. *Henri Matisse Engraving*, 1900–03
    Drypoint
    5⁵⁄₁₆ x 7⁷⁄₈ in. (15.1 x 20.1 cm.) D.1
    Gift of Mrs. Bertram Smith

15/30.
Henri Matisse

2. *The Weeper,* 1900–03
   Drypoint
   5⅞ x 3¹³⁄₁₆ in. (14.9 x 7.9 cm.) D.7
   Purchase Fund

3.   *Small Black Woodcut,* 1906
       Woodcut
       12¼ x 8⁷⁄₁₆ in. (31.2 x 21.5 cm.) D.319
       Abby Aldrich Rockefeller Fund

HM.

Henri Matisse
40/50

4. *Large Nude,* 1906
   Lithograph
   11$\frac{3}{16}$ x 9$\frac{15}{16}$ in. (28.4 x 25.3 cm.) D.403
   Gift of Abby Aldrich Rockefeller

5.   *The Large Woodcut*, 1906
      Woodcut
      18¾ x 15 in. (47.5 x 38.1 cm.) D.317
      Gift of Mr. and Mrs. R. Kirk Askew, Jr.

6. *Woman's Head, Eyes Closed,* 1906
    Transfer lithograph
    17⁵⁄₁₆ x 10¹³⁄₁₆ in. (44.0 x 27.5 cm.) D.390
    Gift of Abby Aldrich Rockefeller

7. *Seated Nude, Seen from the Back*, 1913
Transfer lithograph
16⅝ x 10⅜ in. (42.3 x 26.4 cm.) D.412
Gift of Mrs. John D. Rockefeller 3rd

N° 1586   H m 37/50

8.   *Three-quarter Nude, Head Partly Showing,* 1913
        Transfer lithograph
        19¾ x 12 in. (50.3 x 30.5 cm.) D.409
        Frank Crowninshield Fund

25/50H m

9. *Standing Nude, Arms Crossed*, 1915
   Monotype
   6^{15}/$_{16}$ x 5^{1}/$_{16}$ in. (17.6 x 12.8 cm.) D.378
   Frank Crowninshield Fund

10. *Loulou, Distracted,* 1914 – 15
    Etching
    7 1/16 x 5 in. (17.9 x 12.7 cm.) D.50
    Purchase

11.   *Mlle Landsberg* (large plate), 1914
       Etching
       7⅞ x 4⁵⁄₁₆ in. (20.0 x 11.0 cm.) D.33
       Gift of Mr. and Mrs. E. Powis Jones

12. *Margot in a Kimono,* 1915
Etching
$7^{11}\!/_{16}$ x $4^{1}\!/_{4}$ in. (19.6 x 10.7 cm.) D.68
Purchase

8/10
henri mati...

13. *Interior. Young Girl Drawing Fruit*, 1914–15
    Monotype
    3$\frac{13}{16}$ x 5$\frac{7}{8}$ in. (9.7 x 14.8 cm.) D.346
    Gift of Abby Aldrich Rockefeller (by exchange)

14.   *Model Resting*, 1922
        Lithograph
        8¾ x 11¹³⁄₁₆ in. (22.3 x 30.0 cm.) D.416
        Purchase

15.   *Leaning Young Girl by a Flowered Screen*, 1923
        Lithograph
        7 1/16 x 10 5/16 in. (17.8 x 26.0 cm.) D.439
        Lillie P. Bliss Collection

47/60   Henri Matisse

16.   *Arabesque*, 1924
      Transfer lithograph
      19¹⁄₁₆ x 12⁵⁄₈ in. (48.5 x 32.2 cm.) D.449
      Lillie P. Bliss Collection

5/50   Henri Matisse

17. *Large Odalisque in Striped Pantaloons*, 1925
Transfer lithograph
21½ x 17⅜ in. (54.6 x 44.2 cm.) D.455
Nelson A. Rockefeller Bequest

18.   *Nude in an Interior, with Fruit Bowl,* 1926
         Drypoint
         7 1/16 x 5 1/16 in. (18.0 x 12.9 cm.) D.103
         Purchase

19.   *Bust of Woman with Necklace and Bracelet*, 1926
        Etching
        7¹⁄₁₆ x 5 in. (17.9 x 12.7 cm.) D.93
        Purchase

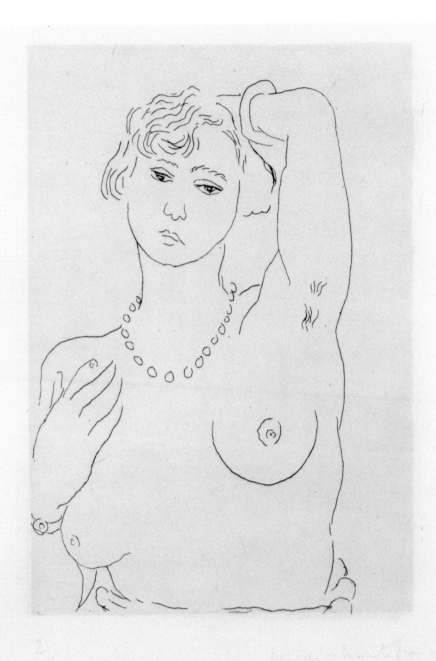

2/15

20. *Upside-down Nude with Stove,* 1929
Lithograph
22 x 18⅛ in. (55.8 x 46.0 cm.) D.500
Gift of Abby Aldrich Rockefeller

21.   *Study of Upside-down Nude,* 1929
       Etching
       6⅝ x 9⅜ in. (16.8 x 23.8 cm.) D.166
       Gift of Mr. and Mrs. E. Powis Jones

2291 Henri Matisse

9/25
Henri-Matisse

22. *Crouching Oriental, Veil on Head*, 1929
Drypoint
6¼ x 4⅞ in. (15.5 x 12.4 cm.) D.155
Purchase

23. *Dancer Reflected in the Mirror,* 1927
    Transfer lithograph
    15⅝ x 11 in. (39.5 x 28.0 cm.) D.490
    Gift of Abby Aldrich Rockefeller

24.   *Reflection in the Mirror,* 1929
        Etching
        10 1/16 x 5 15/16 in. (25.4 x 15.2 cm.) D.116
        Gift of Mrs. Gertrud A. Mellon

25.   *The White Fox*, 1929
       Lithograph
       20⅜ x 14¼ in. (51.8 x 36.2 cm.) D.514
       The Associates Fund

26. *Young Woman with Black Eyes, Staring at an Aquarium,* 1929
Etching
3⅝ x 4⅞ in. (9.2 x 12.4 cm.) D.179
Purchase

2/25

Henri Matisse

27.   *Woman, Thumb on Lips,* 1938
      Linoleum cut
      11 1/8 x 7 13/16 in. (28.2 x 19.9 cm.) D.714
      Gift in memory of Bertha M. Slattery

3/25

Henri Matisse

28.   *Five Female Heads,* 1939
        Aquatint
        2$\frac{1}{16}$ x 9$\frac{3}{4}$ in. (5.1 x 24.8 cm.) D.772
        Peter H. Deitsch Bequest

20/20

Henri Matisse

29. *Self-Portrait, Three-quarter View,* 1948
Lithograph
9 x 7¼ in. (23.0 x 18.3) D.634
Curt Valentin Bequest

matisse

22/25

30.   *Nadia with Sharp Profile,* 1948
        Aquatint
        $16^{15}/_{16}$ x $13^{3}/_{4}$ in. (43.0 x 34.9 cm.) D.810
        Curt Valentin Bequest

H. Matisse
16/215

31.   *Three Heads. To Friendship,* 1951 – 52
      Aquatint
      13⅝ x 10¹⁵⁄₁₆ in. (34.6 x 27.8 cm.) D.827
      Gift of Mr. and Mrs. Armand P. Bartos

H.M.
2/3

CHRONOLOGY

1869
31 December: Henri-Emile-Benoît Matisse born at Le Cateau-Cambrésis.

1882–87
Studies at the lycée Saint-Quentin.

1887–88
Studies law in Paris; returns to Saint-Quentin to become a law clerk.

1890
Begins painting.

1891–92
Abandons law and becomes a student under Bouguereau at the Académie Julian in Paris.

1892
Draws from the antique at the Cour Yvon at the Ecole des Beaux-Arts; begins (unofficially) in Gustave Moreau's class. Attends evening classes at the Ecole des Arts Décoratifs.

1894
Birth of daughter Marguerite.

1895
Passes the entrance examination to the Ecole des Beaux-Arts.

1895
Enters Gustave Moreau's class at the Ecole des Beaux-Arts.

1896
Salon de la Société Nationale des Beaux-Arts accepts four of his paintings and elects him to the society as an associate member.

1898
Marries Amélie Parayre of Toulouse.

1899
Birth of son Jean.

1900
Birth of son Pierre.

1901
Exhibits at the Salon des Indépendants.

1903
First attempts at engraving.

1904
First one-man show, with Ambroise Vollard, Paris.

1905
October: exhibits with the Fauves at the Salon d'Automne.

1906
March: one-man show at the Galerie Druet, Paris, includes drawings and woodcuts. Exhibits at the Salon d'Automne. Meets Picasso through Gertrude and Leo Stein.

1907
Autumn: exchanges paintings with Picasso who is working on *Les Demoiselles d'Avignon*. Admirers organize a school (Académie Matisse) in rue de Sèvres, Paris, where he teaches.

1908
First exhibition in the United States at Alfred Stieglitz's Little Galleries of the Photo-Secession ("291"), New York, shows drawings, watercolors, and prints. December: publishes "Notes d'un peintre."

1911
Exhibits at the Salon des Indépendants.

1913
Participates in the Armory Show in New York.

1914
Rejected from military service.

1918
Exhibits with Picasso at Galerie Paul Guillaume.

1920
Works on the ballet *Le Chant du rossignol* by Diaghilev. Publication of *Cinquante dessins par Henri Matisse* supervised by the artist.

1921
From now on, spends half of the year in Nice and the other half in Paris, until the early 1930s.

1922
Focuses on lithography.

1925
Is made chevalier de la Légion d'honneur.

1927
Awarded First Prize at the Carnegie International Exhibition in Pittsburgh. Exhibits drawings and lithographs at Galerie Bernheim-Jeune.

1929
Concentrates on numerous drypoints, prints, and lithographs.

1930
Commissioned by Albert Skira to illustrate Stéphane Mallarmé's poems. Important retrospective at Galerie Thannhauser in Berlin.

1931
Series of important retrospectives in Paris (Galerie Georges Petit), Basel (Kunsthalle), New York (The Museum of Modern Art). Concentrates on the illustrations to Mallarmé.

1932
Publication of Mallarmé's *Poésies,* with twenty-nine etchings. Exhibition at Pierre Matisse Gallery, New York, of the fifty drawings chosen by Matisse for the 1920 publication *Cinquante dessins.*

1934–35
Focuses on the series of engravings for *Ulysses* by James Joyce.

1939
September: leaves Paris after declaration of World War II. October: returns to Nice.

1940
Legal separation from Madame Matisse.

1941
Begins illustrating *Florilège des amours* by Ronsard. Spring spent in hospital in Lyons recovering from two intestinal operations.

1942
Exchanges paintings and drawings with Picasso. Works on the illustrations for *Poèmes* by Charles d'Orléans.

1943
Publication of *Thèmes et variations* preceded by the text "Matisse-en-France" by Louis Aragon.

1944
Participates in the Salon d'Automne exhibition in celebration of the Liberation. Illustrations for Baudelaire's *Les Fleurs du mal.*

1945
Summer: returns to Paris. Series of exhibitions, including important retrospective at the Salon d'Automne.

1946
Illustrates the letters of Marianna Alcaforado.

1947
Publication of *Jazz* (Tériade) and of *Les Fleurs du mal,* illustrated by Matisse.

1948
Retrospective at the Philadelphia Museum of Art. Publication of *Florilège des amours.*

1949
Retrospective in Lucerne, Musée des Beaux-Arts.

1950
Publication of *Poèmes* by Charles d'Orléans with lithographs by Matisse. Receives highest prize at the 25th Venice Biennale.

1951
Matisse retrospective at The Museum of Modern Art, New York. Publication of Alfred Barr's monograph *Matisse: His Art and His Public.*

1952
Inauguration of the Musée Henri Matisse at Le Cateau-Cambrésis.

1954
3 November: Matisse dies in Nice and is buried at Cimiez.

SELECTED BIBLIOGRAPHY

Barr, Alfred H., Jr. *Matisse: His Art and His Public*. New York: The Museum of Modern Art, 1951.

Breeskin, A.D. "Matisse and Picasso as Book Illustrators." *Baltimore Museum News*, No. 14 (May 1951), pp. 1–3.

Castleman, Riva. *Prints of the Twentieth Century: A History*. New York: The Museum of Modern Art, 1976.

Courthion, Pierre. *Henri Matisse*. Paris: Editions Rieder, 1934.

Diehl, Gaston. *Henri Matisse*. Paris: Pierre Tisné, 1954.

Duthuit, Marguerite. "Introduction," *Henri Matisse, lithographies rares*. Paris: Galerie Berggruen et Cie, 1954.

Duthuit, Marguerite, and Claude Duthuit. *Henri Matisse: catalogue raisonné de l'oeuvre gravé*, in collaboration with Françoise Garnaud, with preface by Jean Guichard-Meili. Paris: 1983.

Elderfield, John, et al. *Matisse in the Collection of The Museum of Modern Art*. New York: The Museum of Modern Art, 1978.

Escholier, Raymond. *Matisse, ce vivant*. Paris: Librairie Arthème Fayard, 1956.

Flam, Jack D. *Matisse on Art*. London: Phaidon Press, 1973.

Fourcade, Dominique. *Henri Matisse: écrits et propos sur l'art*. Paris: Hermann, 1972.

————. "Introduction," *Henri Matisse, dessins et sculpture*. Paris: Centre Georges Pompidou, Musée National d'Art Moderne, 1975.

Gowing, Lawrence. *Matisse*. London: Thames and Hudson, 1979.

Guichard-Meili, Jean. *Henri Matisse, son oeuvre, son univers*. Paris: Fernand Hazan, 1967.

Hahnloser-Ingold, Margrit. "Notes sur l'oeuvre graphique de Henri Matisse," *Henri Matisse, gravures et lithographies de 1900 à 1929*. Pully: Maison Pullierane, 1970.

————. "Matisse graveur," *Henri Matisse, gravures et lithographies*. Fribourg: Musée d'Art et d'Histoire, 1982.

Huyghe, René. *Henri Matisse*. Paris: Flammarion, 1953.

Jacobus, John. *Henri Matisse*. New York: Harry N. Abrams, 1972.

Lambert, Susan. *Matisse Lithographs*. New York: Universe Books, 1982.

Lassaigne, Jacques. *Matisse*. Geneva: Albert Skira, 1959.

Leymarie, Jean. *Henri Matisse*. Paris: 1970.

Lieberman, William S. "Illustrations by Henri Matisse." *Magazine of Art*, No. 44 (December 1951), pp. 308–14.

————. *Etchings by Matisse*. New York: The Museum of Modern Art, 1955.

————. *Matisse: 50 Years of His Graphic Art*. New York: George Braziller, 1956.

Monod-Fontaine, Isabelle. *Matisse: oeuvres de Henri Matisse (1869–1954)*. Paris: Centre Georges Pompidou, Musée National d'Art Moderne, 1979.

Neff, John Hallmark. "Matisse and Decoration: An Introduction." *Arts Magazine*, No. 49 (May 1975), pp. 59–61; (June 1975), p. 85.

Roger-Marx, Claude. "L'Oeuvre gravé d'Henri Matisse." *Arts et métiers graphiques*, No. 34 (1933).

Sachs, Paul J. *Modern Prints and Drawings*. New York: Alfred A. Knopf, 1954.

Schneider, Pierre. *Henri Matisse*, trans. Michael Taylor and Bridget Stevens Romer. New York: Rizzoli International Publications, Inc., 1984.

Woimant, Françoise. "Matisse, graveur et peintre du livre." *La Revue du Louvre*, No. 2 (1970).

EXHIBITION CHECKLIST

All works are from the collection of The Museum of Modern Art. Dimensions are given in inches and centimeters, height preceding width, with composition or plate size for prints and page size for books. "D." refers to Duthuit numbers.

Henri Matisse Engraving, 1900–03
Drypoint
5⁵⁄₁₆ x 7⁷⁄₈ in. (15.1 x 20.1 cm.) D.1
Gift of Mrs. Bertram Smith

Four Nudes, Two Heads, 1900–03
Drypoint
4¾ x 3⅛ in. (12.1 x 7.9 cm.) D.2
Purchase

Two Studies of a Nude, 1900–03
Drypoint
5¹³⁄₁₆ x 4 in. (14.9 x 10.0 cm.) D.5
Purchase

Two Nudes, Two Heads of Children, 1900–03
Drypoint
5⁷⁄₈ x 4 in. (14.9 x 10.0 cm.) D.6
Purchase

The Weeper, 1900–03
Drypoint
5⁷⁄₈ x 3¹³⁄₁₆ in. (14.9 x 9.7 cm.) D.7
Purchase Fund

Two Women in Street Costume, 1900–03
Drypoint
5¹³⁄₁₆ x 3 ¹⁵⁄₁₆ in. (14.8 x 10.0 cm.) D.9
Purchase

The Large Woodcut, 1906
Woodcut
18¾ x 15 in. (47.5 x 38.1 cm.) D.317
Gift of Mr. and Mrs. R. Kirk Askew, Jr.

Small Light Woodcut, 1906
Woodcut
13½ x 10⅝ in. (34.2 x 26.9 cm.) D.318
Abby Aldrich Rockefeller Fund

Small Black Woodcut, 1906
Woodcut
12¼ x 8⁷⁄₁₆ in. (31.2 x 21.5 cm.) D.319
Abby Aldrich Rockefeller Fund

Woman's Head, Eyes Closed, 1906
Transfer lithograph
17⁵⁄₁₆ x 10¹³⁄₁₆ in. (44.0 x 27.5 cm.) D.390
Gift of Abby Aldrich Rockefeller

Crouching Nude, Eyes Lowered, 1906
Transfer lithograph
15½ x 9⅛ in. (39.4 x 23.1 cm.) D.394
Purchase

Crouching Nude in Profile with Black Hair, 1906
Transfer lithograph
16⅝ x 8¾ in. (42.2 x 22.3 cm.) D.395
Larry Aldrich Fund

Pensive Nude in Folding Chair, 1906
Lithograph
14¾ x 10⅝ in. (37.4 x 26.9 cm.) D.396
Given in memory of Leo and Nina Stein

Upside-down Head, 1906
Transfer lithograph
11⅛ x 10¾ in. (28.3 x 27.4 cm.) D.397
Gift of Abby Aldrich Rockefeller

Large Nude, 1906
Lithograph
11³⁄₁₆ x 9¹⁵⁄₁₆ in. (28.4 x 25.3 cm.) D.403
Gift of Abby Aldrich Rockefeller

Three-quarter Nude, Head Partly Showing, 1913
Transfer lithograph
19¾ x 12 in. (50.3 x 30.5 cm.) D.409
Frank Crowninshield Fund

Nude in Rocking Chair, 1913
Transfer lithograph
19 x 11 in. (48.1 x 27.9 cm.) D.410
Gift of Abby Aldrich Rockefeller

Black Eyes, 1913
Transfer lithograph
17⅞ x 12¾ in. (45.3 x 32.6 cm.) D.411
Gift of Mrs. Saidie A. May

Seated Nude, Seen from the Back, 1913
Transfer lithograph
16⅝ x 10⅜ in. (42.3 x 26.4 cm.) D.412
Gift of Mrs. John D. Rockefeller 3rd

Half-length Nude, 1913-14
Drypoint
5¹¹⁄₁₆ x 3¹⁵⁄₁₆ in. (14.5 x 10.0 cm.) D.13
Purchase

Standing Figure, Head Lowered, 1914
Etching
6⁵⁄₁₆ x 2⅜ in. (16.0 x 6.0 cm.) D.28
Abby Aldrich Rockefeller Fund

Utamaro, 1914
Etching
7 x 5⅛ in. (17.9 x 13.0 cm.) D.29
Gift of Abby Aldrich Rockefeller

Mlle Landsberg, (large plate), 1914
Etching
7⅞ x 4⁵⁄₁₆ in. (20.0 x 11.0 cm.) D.33
Gift of Mr. and Mrs. E. Powis Jones

Fanny (Mme D.G.), 1914
Etching
6³⁄₁₆ x 2⅜ in. (16.0 x 6.1 cm.) D.36
Lillie P. Bliss Collection

Portrait of Bourgeat Resembling Vassaux, 1914
Etching
7⅛ x 5¹⁄₁₆ in. (18.0 x 12.8 cm.) D.40
Acquired through the Lillie P. Bliss Bequest

Portrait of Walter Pach, 1914
Etching
6⅜ x 2⅜ in. (16.1 x 6.1 cm.) D.42
Purchase

Matthew Prichard, 1914
Etching
7⅛ x 4³⁄₁₆ in. (18.2 x 12.2 cm.) D.43
Purchase

M. S. Prichard, 1914
Etching
7¹³⁄₁₆ x 5¹³⁄₁₆ in. (19.9 x 14.8 cm.) D.44
Purchase

Loulou, Distracted, 1914–15
Etching
7¹⁄₁₆ x 5 in. (17.9 x 12.7 cm.) D.50
Purchase

Loulou, Backview, 1914–15
Etching
7¹⁄₁₆ x 5¹⁄₁₆ in. (17.9 x 12.8 cm.) D.51
Purchase

Mme Derain, 1914
Etching
3½ x 2⁹⁄₁₆ in. (9.0 x 6.5 cm.) D.57
Gift of Mrs. W. Murray Crane

Interior. Young Girl Drawing Fruit, 1914–15
Monotype
3¹³⁄₁₆ x 5⅞ in. (9.7 x 14.8 cm.) D.346
Gift of Abby Aldrich Rockefeller (by exchange)

Standing Nude, Arms Crossed, 1915
Monotype
6¹⁵⁄₁₆ x 5¹⁄₁₆ in. (17.6 x 12.8 cm.) D.378
Frank Crowninshield Fund

Josette Gris ("Seraphique"), 1915
Etching
5⅞ x 4⁵⁄₁₆ in. (14.9 x 11.0 cm.) D.62
Purchase

Double Portrait of Josette Gris, 1915
Etching
5¹⁄₁₆ x 7¹⁄₁₆ in. (12.9 x 17.9 cm.) D.64
Abby Aldrich Rockefeller Fund

Margot in a Kimono, 1915
Etching
7¹¹⁄₁₆ x 4¼ in. (19.6 x 10.7 cm.) D.68
Purchase

Demetrius Galanis, Three-quarter View, 1915–16
Etching and drypoint
3⁹⁄₁₆ x 2⁹⁄₁₆ in. (9.0 x 6.5 cm.) D.69
Purchase

Demetrius Galanis, "Peasant," 1915–16
Etching and drypoint
5½ x 3⅞ in. (14.0 x 9.9 cm.) D.70
Purchase